TeenageRomance

Teenage Romance
or How to Die of Embarrassment

Delia Ephron
With drawings by Edward Koren

THE VIKING PRESS NEW YORK

First published in 1981 by The Viking Press
625 Madison Avenue, New York, N.Y. 10022

Published simultaneously in Canada by
Penguin Books Canada Limited

LIBRARY OF CONGRESS CATALOGING IN PUBLICATION DATA
Ephron, Delia.
Teenage romance.
1. Adolescence—Anecdotes, facetiae, satire,
etc. 2. Dating (Social customs)—Anecdotes,
facetiae, satire, etc. I. Title.
PN6231.A26E64   818′.5402   81–411
ISBN 0–670–69503–3   AACR1

10 9 8 7 6 5 4

Printed in the United States of America
Set in Linotron Times Roman

For Jerry

Acknowledgments

I interviewed many people, both adults and teenagers, in the course of writing this book. I owe them a special debt of gratitude. They were generous in sharing their experiences and invaluable in helping me recall my teenage life—most of which, I discovered, I had repressed for good reason. Also I would like to thank my friends who provided editorial advice—Ann Banks, Darrell Brock, Betty Anne Clarke, Amy Ephron, Nora Ephron, Deena Goldstone, Charles Kaufman, Peggy Miller, Jamie Wolf, and Judy Wunsch. To my editor, Amanda Vaill, and designer, Beth Tondreau, a special thanks. It was a pleasure to work together. And, finally, to Edward Koren and Lorraine Bodger, my thanks and love.

Contents

TeenageRomance

How to Make a Pass

I'll count to ten and then I'll do it. One, two, three, four, five, six, seven, eight, nine . . . I'll count to twenty. One, two, three, four, five, six, seven, eight, nine, ten, eleven, twelve, thirteen, fourteen, fifteen, sixteen, seventeen, eighteen, nineteen . . . Okay, wait, start over. I'll count to ten and this time I'll definitely do it. One, two, three, four, five, six, seven, eight, nine, ten.

I'm not doing it.

Look, it's no big deal—I get to ten, I do it. One, two, three, four, five, six, seven, eight, nine, onetwothreefourfivesixseveneightnineten —do it! What am I waiting for? What do I think's going to happen? Nothing, right? Right, nothing. Oh yeah, she'll probably slug me. No seriously, calm down. Stop being such a total and complete asshole. She's probably dying for me to do it. I'll never do it. Do it! One, two, three, four, five, six, seven, eight, nine, ten.

Congratulations, I didn't do it. I probably hold the world's record for not doing it.

Okay, relax. Sit back, listen to the music, and relax. Now wait for this song to end and then do it for sure. Great—as soon as this song . . . Okay, the next song. When the next song is over, I have no choice . . .

I'm not doing it.

1

She knows I'm sitting here trying to do it. She's waiting. She probably thinks I'm pathetic. I bet she's laughing. Screw it! Who cares anyway. I don't even like her. She's ugly. She's a dog! Who needs it? I mean, really, who . . .?

One, two, three, four, five, no, wait, start over. This is really it. One . . . two . . . three . . . four . . . five . . . six . . . seven . . . eight . . . nine . . . nine and a half . . . nine and three-quarters, I can't, I absolutely can't, I may be paralyzed.

Onetwothreefourfivesixseveneightnineten!

Shit, I can't do it. I'm going to be sitting here forever counting like a total jerk. I've got to do it. I've got to—one, two, three, four, five, six, seven, hey, I'm doing it! I don't believe it! Hey, I'm really . . . Wow, I'm . . . Wow! *I* am doing it!

How to Hide a Pimple

While casually playing with hair, pull strand across face at pimple level. Secure hair in mouth.

Apply Band-Aid.

Press hand against cheek as if punctuating the expression, "Oh my!"

If pimple is on forehead, wear bangs.

3

Camouflage with make-up, patting it on with index finger.

If pimple is on chin, rest elbow on table top, chin in hand.

If pimple is on upper lip, assume a pensive pose: Arm is bent at elbow, hand rests against chin, fingers are spread apart so pinkie covers pimple.

Make the following calculation: If pimple is on my left side, my date should always be on my right side. Conversely, if pimple is on my right side, my date should always be on my left side.

How to Attend a Slumber Party

ARRIVING

"Hi, look what I brought!" Put down tote bag and take out four record albums while still standing in the doorway. While getting the records out of the bag, pull out shortie pajamas and stuffed animal by mistake. Stuff them back in. Then announce that you just got your ears pierced and show off your earrings. Say that you have to wear real gold earrings or your ears will get infected. Ask where everyone's going to sleep.

On the way to the bedroom, make other inquiries. How many girls are coming? Can you stay up all night? Can you watch television? Is it color? Can you raid the refrigerator? Where's the stereo? Say hello to the mother of the girl who is giving the party and show her your ears. Say that you have to wear real gold earrings or your ears will get infected. Repeat this information to each guest as she arrives.

CHANGING

Do not let anyone see you naked: Face the wall and put top of shortie pajamas on *over* shirt—just slip it over your head, but do not put arms in sleeves. Unbutton shirt under shortie top and remove.

Being certain that your front is still covered, put hands under shortie top, slip bra straps off shoulders, and quickly insert arms into shortie sleeves.

Now your shortie top is on but your bra is hanging around your waist like a belt. If necessary, turn bra around so fastenings are in front. Undo. Crumple bra into ball and stuff into tote bag. Then put shortie bottoms on over your underpants. Notice that one girl is wearing bikini-style underpants. Envy her.

ACTIVITIES

While eating potato chips, pretzels, and Oreos, discuss which comes first, looks or personality. Rank the boys according to best personality and best looks. When one girl mentions a guy that you think is disgusting, say, "Euuuuuuuuuu, you like *him?*" Make the cuckoo sign by circling your finger next to your ear. Say that you think the guy's an ape—personally you don't like them too hairy. Discuss how much hair a guy should have. Say that you were at the beach one time and saw a guy with hair on his back. Hideola. Mention John Travolta as an example of a guy with the right amount of hair.

Announce that if a girl had all the children she could have from now until she couldn't have any more, she'd have forty children. Say that Coke and aspirin make you drunk. Argue about whether, if you use Tampax, you're still a virgin. Read aloud from the *Home Medical Encyclopedia* on the subject of contraception. Give your mother's opinion of the pill. Say that your older sister's done it.

Paint your toenails.

Offer to pierce somebody's ears. Explain that if you put ice on her earlobes, she won't feel a thing.

Dance fast.

Make everyone stop dancing and listen to the next song on the album. Point out the dirty words in the lyrics.

Call up a teacher on the telephone and hang up when he answers.

While you eat pizza and drink Coke, discuss girls in the class who were not invited:

"She has no personality at all."

"Re-tard, re-tard, re-tard, re-tard."

"Oh God, she's so conceited, she thinks she's so great." Imitate the way she walks, fluff your hair, say, "Darlinck," faking an English accent, and extend hand to be kissed. Sit down suavely in chair and cross legs; then decide instead to sit on top of your best friend, who is lying on her stomach, eating pizza. Jump up and down on her until she threatens to throw up.

Outline the proper way to kiss: Lips should be slightly apart, soft and beckoning, not tense. Pucker. Listen to the sound of the word. Pucker. Say it again. Say it several times, really fast—puckerpuckerpuckerpuckerpuckerpucker. Say it slowly—pucker-rrrrrrrrrrrrrrrr. Pucker. Rhymes with you-know-what! Yell out, "Fucker!" and slap hand over mouth. Listen to see if the mother of the girl who is giving the slumber party is going to appear in the doorway. When she doesn't, continue: Can anyone say, "One smart fellow, he felt smart," really fast over and over again. A girl tries and says, "One fart smellow." Point at her—"Ooooo, what you said!"—then return to the subject of kissing. Heads should be tilted slightly to the side so noses don't collide. Tongues . . . Where do the tongues go? You are not sure. Go to the mirror and see what your lips look like in position. Observe the location of the tongue. Moisten lips with tongue to see if you look sexy moistening your lips and if lips look sexy moistened. Check each girl to see whether her lips are positioned correctly for kissing. Tell one girl she's doing it wrong.

Go around the room from girl to girl, classifying lips—thin lips, fat lips, thin lips, fat lips.

Say, "Who here's kissed? Raise your hand." Say, "Who here's frenched?" Look around. Tell a story about how two teenagers with braces kissed and their braces locked. They had to be taken to the hospital to be disconnected. Hug pillow, call it by the name of the boy who is number one on your list. Kiss it, demonstrating proper kissing method—mouth open, head tilted. Hug it tight. Kiss it again, then suddenly hold pillow at arm's length and say to it, "Didn't I tell you to keep your tongue in your mouth? Honestly!" Throw the pillow at a girlfriend. Have a pillow fight.

Put on Bonne Bell moisturizer and pass the bottle around so everyone can put on Bonne Bell moisturizer.

Starting in a whisper and getting louder, chant, "Come, come, come, come, come, come." Have hysterics laughing. Yell, "Who here knows where the egg and the sperm meet?" Draw a picture of a sperm, write "SPERM" under it, say, "Is this yours?" and hand it to the girl next to you.

"They're here!" Shriek and race to the living room window. "Who is it, which ones, ohmyGod, they saw me!"—peek out from behind curtain through window at the boys. Shriek again when one girl grabs

the curtain and pulls it aside so all the girls get seen in their shortie pajamas. Shriek when the boys wind toilet paper around a tree. Throw a girl's bra out the window. Open the door and say, "What do you want?" Have a conversation while just sticking head outside so shortie pajamas don't show.

BEDTIME

"Are you asleep yet?"
"No, are you?"
"No, is she?"
"Can't tell."
"What about her?" Poke her.
"Come on."
Get out of sleeping bag, tiptoe around the room collecting bras. Tiptoe downstairs. Wet bras in sink and place in freezer compartment of refrigerator. On your way back upstairs, carry a pot of water. When the hostess's mother sees you, tell her you're thirsty. Return to the bedroom, put a sleeping girl's hand in the water to see if she will wet her bed.
"Would you guys cut it out!"
Get back in sleeping bag. . . .
"Are you asleep yet?"
"I can't hear you, I'm asleep."
Giggle. . . .
"Are you asleep yet?"
"Yeah, I'm asleep, that's why I'm talking. I always talk in my sleep."

Giggle.

Get out of sleeping bag and walk around the room, eyes closed, arms extended in front of you—you are sleepwalking. Crash into the door.

"Shut up already! I'm trying to sleep!"

Get back in sleeping bag. . . .

"Are you asleep yet? Psst, hey, are you asleep? Are you?" Get out of sleeping bag and whisper in her ear, "Come, come, come, come, come, come, come, come."

How to Go to the Movies

INSTRUCTIONS FOR BOY

At the ticket window, bend knees to appear half a foot shorter and say, "One child." When the ticket seller asks your age, tell her you're twelve. She will inform you that you have to be under twelve. "Oh yeah, I almost forgot, I'm eleven. I'll be twelve next week." Smile at her. "Honest." She doesn't say anything. "Would I lie to you?" She doesn't say anything. "Okay, okay, I'll tell you the truth. I'm a senior citizen. I look young for my age. This isn't my hair. I'm completely bald." Pay the full price.

Note: If the movie is R-rated, and you have to be seventeen or accompanied by an adult, either ask for a ticket while smoking a cigarette or claim to be the son of the person standing behind you in line.

INSTRUCTIONS FOR GIRL

Apologize to your girlfriends for being late but your mom was out of her gourd. Say that you look a mess, hot weather makes your hair frizz—does it look too curly? "Do you believe this!"—show them a pimple on your chin, and ask to borrow a comb—your hair's not

dirty, you just washed it. If your friends compliment you on your
top, inform them it's new, you got it on sale. Tell them where. Tell them
how much it cost. Say that it's damaged, that's why it was so cheap.
Pull it out of your waistband and show your friends the little hole at the
bottom. Stuff it back in and buy ticket.

Enter theater, and when you are certain no usher is watching, open up the side exit door and let the rest of the guys in free.

On your way into the theater, stop at exhibits of coming attractions
and announce in regard to each one whether you want to see it. While
looking at exhibits, check out your reflection in the glass. Notice your
eyes. Are they getting smaller? Wonder if they were that small this
morning. Were they always that small? Ask one of your friends, "Do
my eyes look smaller than usual?"

Grab seats quickly and look behind you. Did an usher notice your friends' illegal entry? Cool—you did it! Turn the palms of your hands up so your friends can slap them. Then, slump down in chair and throw a leg over the seat in front.

When one of your friends returns with popcorn, stuff a handful into your mouth. Chew while you watch an usher in the next aisle. Is he coming in this direction? Worry. Suppose he asks to see your ticket stub. Check to see if yours is in your pocket. Imagine that he asks to see your friends' ticket stubs. They say theirs are lost, and you say that you'll vouch for them, they bought tickets. The usher says, "Are you with them?" and you all get arrested. The police call your mom and inform her that you are an accomplice. You beg her, "Whatever you do, Mom, just don't tell Dad."

Stuff another handful of popcorn into your mouth while you envision yourself in court. The ticket seller is testifying. She remembers you, all right—you're the one who tried to get in for under twelve. Pick pieces of popcorn out of your teeth while you watch the usher walk back up the aisle. Notice that one of your friends keeps looking around nervously. Say, "Relax, man, nobody saw."

After discussing whether it's safe to leave your sweaters on the seats, go to the refreshment stand. Return, remove gum from mouth, and stick it under the armrest. Begin eating popcorn, selecting the most buttered pieces first and being anxious, when you offer popcorn to your friends, that you will get the container back with all the buttered pieces gone. Observe the fingernails of a friend when she takes some popcorn. Why are her fingernails always so clean and yours always so dirty?

Turn around and scan the audience—do you know anyone? Notice three girls sitting two rows away. Yell, "Hey, isn't your name Patti? No, I know, it's Susan," while one of your friends shouts, "Gertrude, Mergatroyd, Rita," and another starts imitating Woody Woodpecker—"Uh-huh-huh-*huh*-huh."

Some guys are yelling at you. Look; no, don't—slide down in seat so head is barely visible. "Who are they?" "Did you see them?"

"Where?" "Unreal!" Cover mouth to conceal giggling. As soon as the yelling stops, crane head over top of the seat to look.

When one of the girls peeks above the seat, call, "Hey, we've got a present for you," and shoot over a spitball. Crack up.

The lights are going down. Slump down again and throw a leg over the seat in front.

As soon as the movie begins, start whispering. "Oh, I've been there"—the city the movie takes place in. You visited it once with your parents. There's the restaurant you had dinner at. Point it out. Give your opinion of the leading man's eyes, the leading man's body. Is he sexy? What do you think of the leading lady's wardrobe? Give the people behind you a dirty look when they tell you to be quiet.

Make loud cracks commenting on the action. In sexy scenes, squeal in a falsetto, "It's love, I know it's love. Take me, Walter, take me." And, "Oh my goodness, I forgot my panties." Lust after the leading lady's breasts. Say you'd like to get her in a dark alley. Add, could you stuff it in her. Put your hand under your arm and squeeze it to make a fart noise. Your friend says, "Now do it with your hand." Burp. If you are sitting in the balcony, throw popcorn container over the railing down to the main floor.

When you hear a guy shriek, "Oh my goodness, I forgot my panties," look over to see if it's those guys, the ones who were yelling at you before. One of them burps really loud—"Oh, gross." Giggle; then look behind you to see if an usher is coming to get them.

16

In a moment of suspense, jump out of seat into friend's lap. Say, "Mind if I keep you company?" to your friend, and, "Oh hello, am I in your way, pardon me," to the people behind you, whose view of the screen you just obliterated. Stick a finger in your nose and hold it there so they see it. Remove finger, wave at them, remove self from friend's lap, and return to seat.

Cover face with hands—the movie is getting scary. Alternate between keeping your fingers close together so you can't see the screen at all and spreading fingers apart so you see fragments of the action. Whisper to a friend, "Tell me when it's over."

As the usher walks past your row down the aisle, remove knees from seat in front of you and sit up.

"What?" Look up. The usher is pointing his flashlight at your leg, which is flung over the seat. Sit up. Deny that you were the person yelling things out. Ask your friends to confirm it. No, you do not want to leave. Act offended. Insist that the noise came from over there, and point across the theater.

Watch the usher. Is he going to kick those guys out? Are you sure you don't know them?

As soon as the usher leaves, throw your leg back over the seat. Turn a palm up so a friend can slap it.

When the usher walks back up the aisle past your row, slump back down and brace knees against the seat in front. Then, notice a couple necking in the next row. Point them out.

The second the movie is over, split, weaving quickly up the aisle through the people.

Walk slowly up the aisle backwards to catch the final credits. On the way out, notice the coming attractions again and name the ones you really want to see. Stop at posters for the movie you just saw. Look at photographs of scenes from the movie. Point out actors you especially liked and which scenes were your favorites. Check your reflection in the glass. Say, "God, my hair's a frizz-ball," and ask to borrow a comb. Look closely at your eyes. Are they smaller or not? Say that you'd like to see the movie again and leave the theater, combing your hair as you walk.

18

How to Have a Crush

Dear Diary,

Remember I told you I wish I could find someone I really like. Well, diary, da-da, da-da, I have!!!!!!!! He's in my French class so I guess I was wrong—French won't be my most boring, worst class after all. His name is Jeffrey Dobkin. Oh diary, you should see him. Brownish hair, taller than me (very important), blue eyes. I noticed him right away because who wouldn't! He's really popular. I mean really, really popular. Compared to him, I'm practically a zero in popularity. But when I first saw him close up, I didn't think I would like him. He just didn't seem like my type. But then I started thinking about him more and more and yesterday during algebra, which is my class after French, I was thinking about him and I just knew. Diary, I'm in love. Do you think that's weird?

DD,

Yesterday I asked if you thought it was weird that I'm in love. I didn't really explain. I've been thinking a lot about that and I guess I mean weird because it just happened. One minute I thought he was cute and the next I was in love. I guess that's the way love works. Today in class I kept looking at Jeffrey the whole time. I couldn't take my eyes off him. Fortunately he didn't know because he sits closer to the front than me so I was looking at the back of his head. Fortunately!!!!!!! I guess if I could have one wish come true this whole year it would be that Jeffrey would like me.

DD,

I have found his locker. Jeffrey's of course. Dear, gorgeous, beautiful, scrumptious Jeffrey, man of my dreams, homme de mes rêves as the Français say. It's on the second floor next to the boys' lavatory. How convenient (hee hee).

DD,

At lunch today, I told Judy about Jeffrey. I swore her to secrecy. Even though she knows who he is, she wanted to see him so we made this circle. We walked from the cafeteria through the main hall to the language lab, up to the second floor, down the hall past you-know-who's locker, and down to the first floor again. After we had walked around three times, he was there. I said, "Don't look now but there

he is," and she looked!!!!!!!!!!!!!!! I could have died. He was looking
right at us!

Judy says Jeffrey is definitely not her type. Her type is Mr. Debold,
the history teacher.

DD,

Right now I am eating yogurt and you can guess why. Dr. Meyrowitz again. There is only one good thing about going to Dr. Meyrowitz and that's missing sixth period. Today he screwed the wires soooooo tight—excuse me, diary, I did not mean to spill yogurt on you. Anyway—surprise, surprise—Dr. Meyrowitz put it off again. First he said he would take my braces off before Christmas. Then February. Now April. In April, I bet he says September. I could cry. Weep, weep. No, seriously, I hate my braces. I look disgusting in them. With my luck, I'll probably look disgusting when they come off, too. Suppose Dr. Meyrowitz takes my braces off and my teeth are all rotten underneath. Suppose there are only little black things like worms where my teeth were. That would really be disgusting. Today I figured out that if I open my mouth, unhook the rubber band from the bottom brace but leave it hooked to the top brace, pull back and release, I can shoot rubber bands across the room. In study hall, I shot rubber bands out of my mouth and hit the page numbers in my book. Not bad.

Oh well, gotta stop. My hand is getting tired.

P.S. Jeffrey wasn't in school today.

DD,

Jeffrey is running for class veep. I hope he wins. I'll vote for him, that's for sure. Guess what? I'm not positive but I think today in class Jeffrey might have noticed me. He looked over when I conjugated aller. I got so nervous that I almost forgot what comes after tu vas and it's practically the same! I could feel my face getting red and I'm glad that no one knew why. Afterward, I was imagining that when class was over, Jeffrey and I would end up walking through the door at the same time and he would say, "Hi," and I would say, "Hi." Then he would say that he really wanted to talk to me 'cause he noticed me in class. His eyes would look right at me. I'd say something like "Oh really?" like I didn't know he'd noticed me. I don't know—the whole idea was dumb 'cause nothing happened.

DD,
   I hate my legs.

DD,
   Judy slept over, and you know what?—we called Jeffrey! We didn't say who we were or anything. Judy did most of it. Well, first I dialed but his father answered so I hung up fast. I couldn't believe it—his father! Then Judy said she'd do it. She made this really sexy voice by holding her nose and said, "Hello, Jeffrey, this is Marilyn, remember me?" and then she started laughing so hard she couldn't talk so I grabbed the phone and slammed it down. Then she called again!!!!!!!!!!!!!! This time she said, "Is this Jeffrey Dobkin speaking?" and when he said yes, we both shouted, "Jeffrey, we want your body." We had total and complete hysterics. We couldn't stop laughing. After that she called back one more time but his father answered and said to stop calling. I wondered if he was going to trace the call and find out it was us!!!!!!!!!!!
   I'm so glad Judy is my best friend.

DD,

Judy believes in reincarnation. She read this book about this woman who started talking German one day for no reason. I mean she wasn't German and she hadn't taken it in school. So after her husband thought she was crazy, he took her to this doctor who gave her a shot so she would talk in her sleep. The lady talked in German and the doctor said that everything she said was true as though she'd lived in Germany in the 17th century.

I wonder who I was in my former life. Probably a rock. Judy says there are clues. Habits like twirling your hair or even favorite foods could be passed on from your other life. That means Judy was probably Chinese 'cause she loves egg rolls (just kidding!). I wonder what Jeffrey was. A prince, sans doute. Maybe a frog (get it?). Maybe a Frito (ha ha). Diary, you may have noticed that I can never start anything without ending up back at Jeffrey. It's hopeless. In class I noticed that he has this really beautiful hair on his arms. Sort of golden. Oh Jeffrey, I wish you sat in bed thinking about me the way I do about you.

DD,

I am so unhappy. Tonight I just stayed in my room, lay on my bed, and cried. I guess this is what love is—always waiting, always hoping, never getting. Oh Jeffrey, why don't you know what I feel? If I could just talk to you. Just talk, that's all I ask (well, maybe not all). I have to find a way to reach you. I have to!!!! How!!?!?!??

DD,

Today Judy and Denise were over and we were discussing Sheila Gardner. (Lately Denise has been my other best friend—well, Judy is my absolutely first best friend; then comes Denise.) We were trying to figure out why Sheila is so popular. One reason is she doesn't talk behind people's backs and she is always laughing and smiling. She looks really, really friendly. The trouble is, if I smile, my braces show. Besides, diary, there's this other problem that I have been meaning to discuss with you. When I was looking in the mirror, I noticed that when I smile a regular-sized smile, my gums show really a lot. It looks revolting to show all this pink stuff around my teeth. So after my braces come off, I'm going to have to smile partway as much as possible so my gums show less. Until then, I should probably not smile at all. I could try being a mysterious type. Like the Mona Lisa, I could smile keeping my lips together but just making the ends of my lips go up. It would be as though I were from a foreign country or had this really amazing thought in my head. That might help with guys. Also I could slouch more and let my hair grow longer. I wonder if Jeffrey would like me then? The truth is I'm probably a hopeless case.

DD,

Happy Valentine's Day. I slipped this really neat card into Jeffrey's locker. On the outside it says, "Hey, lover, gimme a break." There's this picture of a bird in a cage. Then you open it, and it says, "Be my Valentine," and the bird flies out of the cage with a heart in its mouth. I signed it "Guess who?"

26

DD,

I've been thinking. I absolutely have to talk to Jeffrey. If I could only talk to him—I bet we have a million things in common. Today, when I came down to the cafeteria for lunch, I saw Jeffrey on the stairs. He was talking to this other kid but I figured that when he was done he would come down to the cafeteria. So I waited at the beginning of the lunch line. I tried to look like I was studying the menu, like I couldn't decide what to eat. I even said, sort of out loud, "What should I eat?" in case it seemed strange that I was standing there. Then, when Jeffrey took a tray, I took the one after him. He had a Sloppy Joe and four milks. I was going to say something about how many milks because I thought it would be a good way to be casual, but I didn't.

DD,

You may have noticed that I have been mentioning Sheila Gardner. Well, I can't keep secrets from you, diary. There's a reason. I think Jeffrey likes her. I'm practically positive because today I heard that she's going to be his campaign manager. I saw them together in the hall and she called him Dob, though I guess that doesn't mean anything 'cause that's what everyone calls him. I don't blame him for liking her. I would too if I were Jeffrey. Her hair's always perfect and so are her clothes. Also her skin is completely without pimples. I can tell just from looking at her that she can always think of something to say, no matter what. Goodnight, dear diary, I'm depressed. Je ne peux pas écrire un autre mot.

DD,

Today Judy and I were walking down the hall toward algebra. Jeffrey was at the drinking fountain talking to this other guy, Tod. Even though I wasn't thirsty, I said, "Excuse me, can I have a drink?" Jeffrey moved aside so I could get to the fountain. He smiled at me. Oh diary, you should see his teeth. Perfect. All in a row, sooooooooo white. Even Dr. Meyrowitz would be impressed! I started to smile back but remembered my braces just in time. Isn't that great! I did just what I planned—I kept my lips together but made the ends go up. I think I looked really friendly but also suave. I hope, I hope, I hope. Anyway, later in French, Jeffrey looked like he remembered me as the girl at the drinking fountain. I am making an impression! Hurrah.

DD,

Judy came over after school. "Guess what?" she said, and showed me her new bra—a B! I couldn't believe it. I'm going to spend the rest of my life an A—I know it. Why does Judy have all the luck? A B! I can't stand it. I want a B so badly. If I could only have a B, I'd be the happiest person. I'd never complain. That's all I want—just a B. I'd give anything. Oh please, I want a B so badly. Please, please, please. Diary, if I could have a B, I cross my heart, I'd never ask for anything again. I wouldn't even mind about my legs.

DD,

Today we had an assembly for election speeches and you wouldn't believe Jeffrey. He was so funny. Everyone was cracking up. He stood up and said, "A-students, B-students, C-students, D-students, and my friends." He's going to win, I know it. While he was up there, I pretended that he was just talking to me and no one else. Sheila did his nomination speech. She took this poem, "The Raven," and she changed all the words to be about class veep. At the end of each verse, where it says, "Quoth the raven, 'Nevermore,'" she said, "Quoth the raven, 'Jeffrey Dobkin.'" Everyone was really impressed. She wasn't even nervous. I wish I was like her. Anyway, all through French I was imagining that I would go up to Jeffrey after class and say, "Good luck, I really hope you win," but I couldn't. Oh Jeffrey, I wish you knew that I was alive.

DD,

I finally figured out Jeffrey's entire schedule. It took ages. I knew that when I was going to gym, he was coming from gym. Plus French—that's two. But I didn't have the other four. Judy said she saw him coming out of Mrs. Weber's English class second period. That leaves algebra, which he has first period just above where I have general science. It's really neat because if I get to school early, I can hang out near his class and pretend I am looking for someone, not him, until he comes and still get to science on time. The other two—

Denise has social studies with him and then there's study hall. I made this chart that shows all the periods and where he is and where I am. Judy thinks we should be spies and follow him for one whole day without his knowing it. Oops, I forgot, it's Judi. She changed her spelling. It's her new identity with her B bra. Lucky her.

DD,

Judi and I made this pact. First she pricked her finger, and then I pricked mine. We pressed our fingers together so the blood got all mixed up. That means we'll be friends forever.

DD,

Jeffrey won. I knew he would. He was really the best, everyone thought so. But oh, diary, I could die, I did the dumbest thing. Madame Flynn gave me the test papers to hand back and when I gave Jeffrey his, I said congratulations. I meant about the election but probably he thought it was about his test. Oh God, I feel like such a jerk. I wanted to disappear the moment I said it. He must think I'm totally dumb. I don't believe I did that! I finally got up my nerve to say something to him and look what happens. I should just keep my big trap shut. I tried not to cry in school but when I got home— buckets. I wish I didn't like him. I wish I hated him. Oh why did I do that! He probably thought I looked at his test paper, or maybe he didn't know what I was talking about. He said thanks but he must still think I'm a jerk. If I could only explain! Oh Jeffrey, I want to talk to you so much. Oh, this is dumb—one thing's for sure, when I talk I mess it up. I feel awful, diary. I really hate love. If this is it, I don't want it, I really don't. Goodnight, diary. This is your best friend with a broken heart signing off.

How to Talk to Your Mother

You are about to leave the house:
"Where are you going?"
"Out."
"Out where?"
"Just out."
"Who are you going with?"
"A friend."
"Which friend?"
"Mom, just a friend, okay? Do you have to know everything?"
"I don't have to know everything. I just want to know who you're going out with."
"Debby, okay?"
"Do I know Debby?"

"She's just a friend, okay?"
"Well, where are you going?"
"Out."

You have just come home:
"Hi, Mom, did anyone call?"
"You did get one call, but I forgot to ask who it was."
"Male or female?"
"Male."
"And you didn't ask! Thanks, Mom, thanks a lot, I really appreciate it. For all I know it was the most important phone call of my life!"

You have just hung up the telephone:
"Who was that, dear?"
"Can't a person have some privacy once in a while!"

You are having a party Saturday night. Your mother has just announced that she expects the guests to stay out of the bedrooms:
"Why?"
"I'd just prefer it."
"Why don't you say it, Mom—SEX. You think everytime two people walk into a room and close the door they're having sexual intercourse. That's what you think, isn't it? Honestly, it's totally ridiculous."

34

"It's not that, it's—"

"You don't trust me."

"That's not true."

"You don't. You don't trust me. How do you think that makes me feel?" Look her straight in the eye. "Mom, you have my word—nothing is going to happen."

"I'm sorry, I can't allow it."

"Can't allow it! Can't allow it!!!! It's my house too, you know, I live here. I have rights! You really don't trust me, that's what it's about, isn't it, you don't trust me. That's terrible. You don't even trust your own kid. God, I don't believe it—a mother who doesn't trust her own kid. Just think about that, Mom, just think about it."

Your mother has just put dinner on the table:
"Oh, Mom, I meant to tell you, I'm a vegetarian."

You have just finished eating dinner:
"May I please be excused? I'm so full I could barf."

You are upset about something that happened at school. Furthermore, you can't find the can opener. Your mother walks into the kitchen:
"What's wrong?"
"Nothing!" Slam the drawer closed.

"What do you mean, 'nothing'? Then why are you slamming drawers?"

"I am not slamming drawers!" Slam another.

"Sweetheart, what's the matter?"

"Will you get off my back! Just lay off, leave me alone, all right? Nothing is wrong! Nothing is wrong! Nothing is wrong! NOTHING IS WRONG! Shit, you're driving me nuts. There's absolutely no peace in this house!!!!!!!!!!" Burst into tears, go to your room, slam the door, and turn on the stereo.

Walk into the house, go to your room, close the door, and turn on the stereo. Your mother knocks:

"Hi, where've you been?"

You do not answer. Fiddle with the stereo, adjusting the balance.

"Would you turn that down while I'm trying to talk to you?"

Turn it down, very slightly.

"I said, 'Turn the music down'!"

Shut it off. Cross your arms in front of your chest, and exhale loudly, appearing exasperated and bored at the same time. "Yes?"

"Whenever I try to talk to you, you're busy. You just come home to eat and sleep. You treat this house like a hotel. Would it be too much trouble, when you arrive home, to come in and say hello?"

"Hello. Now are you satisfied?"

You and your mother are at the movies. Your mother thinks something that just happened on the screen is very funny:

"Mom, cut it out. Stop laughing so loud. Everyone's looking."

It's Saturday night and your mother is insisting that you be home by midnight:

"Oh, Mom, come on. Nobody gets home that early, nobody! Do you want me to be the only kid in the entire group that has to leave early? The only one who can't stay out! Do you? Do you want me to ruin everyone else's time because I have to leave because my mom doesn't trust me while everyone else's mom does? Is that what you want? Is it? Great, just great. You're really getting impossible, you know that? You've changed, Mom, you have. You never listen, you never try to understand. You just give orders—do this, do that. This isn't the army, you know. You're not my boss!"

"Until you're eighteen years old, I am your boss whether you like it or not."

"Oh, Mom, come on, just this once. Please. Pretty please. I never have any fun, I really don't. You never let me do anything I want. Never. If you had your way, I'd be in jail. You know, you're ruining my life. Probably no one will ever invite me anywhere again as long as I live. I'll probably never have another date. I'll spend the rest of my life in my room. Is that what you want? Is it? I hope you're happy, I really hope so. Maybe I won't even go. I mean, what's the point? I have to come home before the party's even started."

You have just used the word "shit":
"I've asked you to watch your language!"
"Who do you think I learned it from?"

Your mother went out for dinner. She has just returned home:
"Hi, Mom, how was the food?"

"Gross."
"Oh Mom, stop trying to act cool."

"Did you clean up your room?"
"Not yet—I will." . . .
"Did you clean up your room?"
"In a minute." . . .
"Did you clean up your room?"
"Give me a break already, I said I'll clean it." . . .
"Did you clean up your room?"
"Cripes, can't you leave me alone for a change? I said I'll do it, I'll do it." . . .
"Did you clean up your room?"
"What?"
"Did you clean up your room?"
"What?"
"DID YOU CLEAN UP YOUR ROOM?"
"You don't have to yell. I'm not deaf, you know. Why don't you calm down. You know, Mom, you always tell me not to shout and then you practically burst a blood vessel. How can I clean up my room with you breathing down my neck? I'll be done in ten minutes—just lay off!" . . .
"Did you clean up your room?"
"Almost." . . .
"Did you—good grief, look at this! You haven't even started yet!

38

Okay, until your room is cleaned up, you're not going out. Is that understood?"

"Fine, I won't go out. Who cares anyway."

It's a school night and you want to go out:
"Did you do your homework?"
"Mom, that homework is completely dumb."
"It may be dumb but did you do it?"
"Sort of."
"What do you mean, sort of?"
"I mean I didn't do it, is that what you want to hear! Is it? Look, Mom, it's my homework, right? If I don't do it, I get the bad grade, right?"
"Fine, but if you want to go out, you'd better do it."
"IT'S MY LIFE! If I want to fuck it up, I WILL!!!!! Besides, Mom, you know, I can go out—you can't stop me."

You have just returned from school:
"How'd you do on the science test?"
"Can't you ever stop asking me questions!"
"I really think that's uncalled for. If I ask, you tell me I'm prying. If I don't ask, you say I'm not interested. I can't win."
"That's right, Mom, you can't."

How to Hang Out

Go to the airport and pretend to greet people.
Drive past a guy's house and see if he's home.
Smoke a cigarillo.
Blow up fifty condoms and sit in a room full of balloons.
Paint a Tampax with red nail polish, put it on the sidewalk, and see what people do when they walk by.
Break pencils with one hand.
Light a match with one hand while the match is still attached to the pack.
Speak in a fake foreign language.
Blow smoke rings.
Loosen the tops of salt shakers before leaving a restaurant.
Take out the car before you have a license.
Go to the movies wearing swim fins and a mask.
Walk down the school hallway with a notebook ring in your nose.
Take a date to a drive-in, and when she goes to the ladies' room, move the car to a new location.
Have a séance.
Find *The Joy of Sex* in your parents' bedroom and read it.
Direct traffic.

Stand near the boys' lavatory and see how long it takes guys to go to the bathroom.

Drive around counting restaurants. Eat in the hundredth one you see.

Prick holes in the bottoms of Dixie cups.

Glue a dollar to the classroom floor and watch kids try to pick it up.

See how many times you can come.

Put little "take-out" packages of mustard and catsup on the sidewalk and step on them.

Look up "penis" in the *Guinness Book of World Records.*

Read the letters in your sister's bureau drawer.

How to Attend Social Studies Class

ATTENTION ALL STUDENTS. BECAUSE OF THE WEATHER WE WILL OBSERVE A RAINY-DAY SCHEDULE.

"Boooooooooooooooooooooooooooooo."

STUDENTS WITH SECOND-PERIOD CLASSES ON THE SECOND FLOOR AND MEZZANINE OF THE MAIN BUILDING AND IN THE NORTH BUILDING, ALL FLOORS, GO TO LUNCH AT ELEVEN FORTY-FIVE AND THEN RETURN TO THEIR SECOND-PERIOD CLASSES.

"What?"
"What floor is this?"
"What did he say?"

STUDENTS WITH SECOND-PERIOD CLASSES ON THE THIRD AND FIRST FLOORS OF THE MAIN BUILDING AND IN THE GYMNASIUM GO TO LUNCH AT TWELVE-THIRTY AND AFTER LUNCH PROCEED TO THEIR THIRD-PERIOD

43

CLASSES. LUNCHTIME MEETINGS OF THE FRENCH CLUB, SPQR, YOUNG LAWYERS, AND CHESS CLUB ARE CANCELED. STUDENTS SHOULD REMEMBER TO RETURN ALL OVERDUE LIBRARY BOOKS.

"What *floor* is this?"
"Did you hear that? I didn't hear that."
"Third, dummy."
"Chess, chess, chest, chest, CHEST!!!"

All right, class, that's the bell.

Race to the center of the room, do a fast dance, wiggling hips back and forth for a split second, and race back to seat. Raise your hand. "Did you finish correcting the tests?"
"Are we going to have a test this week?"
"Is it going to be true or false?"
"Is it going to be multiple choice?"
"Will there be a map?"
"A test. Oh no, a test!"
"Did she say when? Did you say when? When?"
"Can I change my seat?"
Drop books on floor.
Drop books on floor.
Drop books on floor.
Drop books on floor. Open compact and check hair.

May I have your attention. I'm waiting . . .
I'm passing out forms for you to fill out. They're from the guidance

office. Print your last name, then your first name, address, and phone
number.

"Do we use pen or pencil?"
"Do we put last name first or first name first?"

I don't care what you use. I said last name, then first name.

"What? What did you say?"
"She said last name first."
"What?"
"Could I start over? I made a mistake."
"Do we use pen or pencil?"

I said I don't care. Use whatever you want.

"I forgot my last name."
"It's Jerk. Could I go to my locker? I forgot my pen."
"Do we fill in the date?"

No. Yes, fill in the date.

"Do we fill in the date?"
"Where? I don't see where we're supposed to write."
"What's the date?"

The date is February twelfth. It's on the blackboard. Don't fill in the
boxes. That's for the office. Yes?

45

"Can I sharpen my pencil?"

No.

"Do we fill in the boxes?"
"Uh-oh, I made a boo-boo."
"Do I write today's date where it says date?"
"My pencil broke. Does anyone have another pencil?"

Do not fill in the boxes. The date is on the blackboard.

"What do we put where it says grade level?"
"Kindergarten, dodo."
"What? What did you say about the boxes?"
"Mine's a mess. Could I start over?"
"She said don't fill them in."

Where it says grade level, put nine. As soon as you are finished, pass the forms to the front of your row, then pass them down.

"Would you repeat that?"

I said when you are finished, pass the forms to the front, then pass them down. Yes?

"Did you finish correcting the tests yet?"

46

No, I said I did not. Do I have everyone's? Okay, open your books to page 184.

"I forgot my book. Can I share?"

Yes.

"What page? I didn't hear."
"One eighty-four."
"One eighty-four?"

One eighty-four.

"Oops, wrong book."

Page 184 at the top of the page. Will the person listening to the transistor radio turn it off.

"Who?"
"Who?"
"Who?"
"Who?"

Mind your own business. He knows who I mean. Who would like to read the first paragraph out loud? Okay, go ahead. Will everyone listen.

Spin your pen on your desk.

Jiggle your leg.

Write your boyfriend's name. Yawn.

Fan yourself with the flap of your book.

With the pen, trace the veins on your wrists so there are blue lines running up your arm. See if the pen can write on your fingernails. If possible, take pen apart. If possible, click it. Stick pen in ear. Then stick pencil in other ear and poke the guy in front of you: You have an arrow through your head. Put pen in sock and scratch ankle.

Silently mouth the words "Did you do number six in geometry?" to a kid across the room. She doesn't understand. Mouth it again. Mouth it slower. She still can't read your lips. Mouth, "Never mind."

Write your boyfriend's name in capital letters. Write it entirely lower case. Write it changing the slant of your handwriting. Ink in the centers of the letters. Change the dots on the *i*'s to circles. Draw a heart around his name. Admire it, then obliterate it, scribbling over. Start again—write your first name with his last name. Write your first name and his first name with his last name.

Doodle, using your jeans as the paper.

Do you agree with that?

"No. Wait—what did you just say?"

"Where are we?"

"I mean yes. Yes."
      "Can I be excused? I have to go to the orthodontist."
   "Where *are* we?"

The answer is no.

   "That's what I meant."
      "Oh, page 185, ah-so, ah-so."

I hope everyone understands. Candidates for President are elected by delegates, not by the people themselves. In states where there are primaries, voters elect delegates who support the candidates of the voters' choice. In states where there are no primaries, the parties elect the delegates and then candidates lobby to get the vote of these delegates. What parties am I talking about?

Chew your eraser.
   Click your pen.
      Take hand lotion out of your purse and rub some on your hands. Pass it to the girl sitting next to you.
         Take some lotion; pass it back.

Democratic and Republican!

Listen to your stomach growl. Hope that nobody hears. Do not look around.

Put head down on desk and go to sleep.
Clean nails with the point of a compass.
Drop comb on floor; retrieve it with your foot.

Can anyone run for President?

"No."

What are the qualifications?

"Can I go to the bathroom?"
"An American."
"Is this going to be on the test?"

An American citizen, but what else?

"Born here."
"Can I go to the bathroom?"

How old does he have to be?

"Thirty-five."
"Forty."
"Sixty-nine."
"I didn't say that—he said that."

Do you have a problem?

"Yeah, mental."
"He's got diarrhea of the mouth!"
"Can I go to the bathroom?"

Yes, hurry up. According to the Constitution, a candidate for President must be thirty-five years of age and a native-born American. Of course there are many other qualifications required by the voters, but we'll get to that. Who can explain the word I've written on the blackboard?

"A plant."

If you want to say something, raise your hand. The word is "caucus," not "cactus." A political caucus is quite simply—is everyone paying attention? You're going to be asked this on the test—a caucus is a meeting of party members or delegates. Parties hold caucuses to poll members on subjects of vital interest and to select delegates. Delegates hold caucuses—they caucus, as we say—to decide which candidate to support.

Stretch, sticking legs out in front of you as far as possible. Check out a girl across the room. What do you think of her? So-so. Look out the window. Wish that you were out there instead of in here. Check the clock. Read the detention list on the blackboard. Look at the teacher's legs. Imagine that your hands are on her ankles. They are moving up her legs, past her calves, lifting her skirt, slowly, slowly, higher, higher, higher. You have an erection.

Do delegates from a state always support the same candidate?

Sit up straight and tuck it in—move as close to the desk as possible.

Does anyone have a different opinion?

Think about baseball.

Anyone else?

Think about ice cream.

Anyone else?

Think about the real ugly cashier in the school cafeteria.

All right, class, that's the bell. Your homework assignment is on the blackboard.

You do not get up. You put on your jacket while sitting in your seat. Then, very slowly, stand up and walk down the aisle, holding your notebook in front, very carefully placed.

Remember, it's a rainy-day schedule.

"Booooooooooooooooooooooo."
"Do we go to third period after lunch or come back here?

"Third."

"Did you say third? Did she say third?"

"Will our tests be corrected tomorrow?"

"Will our tests be corrected tomorrow?"

"Will our tests be corrected tomorrow?"

"Will our tests be corrected tomorrow?"

"Will our tests be corrected tomorrow?"

55

How to Pick Up a Girl

With a friend, slide into a booth in a coffee shop. Say, "Don't look now," and flip thumb in the direction of the next booth. Two girls are sitting there.

When the waitress comes to take your order, lie to her, explaining that your friend doesn't speak English. To prove it, address friend in your own invented version of a foreign language. He answers in his version. Speak to him again in gibberish. He answers in gibberish. Translate for the waitress: "He'll have a cheeseburger and an order of fries." Converse with friend again and translate: "He'll have a Coke." Look over to see if the girls are paying attention. Tell the waitress that your friend is Norwegian.

When the waitress leaves, sit sideways so you can look into the girls' booth. "Uh, excuse me, could I talk to you a minute. My friend here's from Norway. He doesn't speak any English. His name is Hans. He's been just a week on foreign soil. He doesn't know any Americans and he'd really appreciate making your acquaintance." They don't say anything. Turn to your friend and say, "They don't believe me"—then use gibberish to make the same point. Your friend replies in gibberish. You answer him. The girls ignore you.

"Look, is this any way to treat a guest in your country?

"Okay, okay, I'll tell you the truth. He's not really from Norway.

He's an American of Norwegian descent. No kidding. I know that comes as a shock to you." The girls refuse to pay attention. They are holding up their menus to hide their faces.

"Uh, excuse me"—tap one of the girls on the shoulder. "My friend here's in love with you. He's too embarrassed to tell you himself. He's madly in love. He walked in here, took one look, and fell. He'll die if you don't talk to him. He will! He'll die. He's already got a bad cough. Look, you're breaking his heart.

"Okay, okay, I'll tell you the truth. He's not exactly madly in love with you. He's just dying to meet you. He thinks you're gorgeous. He thinks you're the most beautiful girl he's ever seen." She looks around the coffee shop so she doesn't look at you. She is sucking in her cheeks to avoid laughing.

"Uh, excuse me"—tap her again. "My friend here's wearing Fruit of the Loom underwear. What do you wear?

"Okay, okay, I'll stop fooling around. Haven't I seen you two someplace before? I know that sounds like a line but it's really not. I think I know you." Mention several cities that you've never been to. Ask if they know the names of some people you know. Ask what school they go to, where they live. They don't answer.

Beg: "Look, please talk to us, please. You're gorgeous—I've never seen anyone like you. Haven't I met you somplace before? Oh, come on, why not?" Turn back in booth and face friend.

Start to eat. Then get up and walk past their table. Suddenly bend, twist, and fall to the floor. Clutch ankle. Moan. Use their table to pull yourself into a standing position and then collapse into their booth. Say, "Can I sit here a minute while my ankle heals?" They are giggling. "Mind if my friend brings over my cheeseburger so it doesn't get cold?"

Your friend comes over with the food and sits down. He apologizes for your behavior, saying, "Don't mind my friend here, he's just nuts." They laugh. You can tell they think he's really good-looking. They think he's much better looking than you. Yeah, he's got the looks, you've got the mouth. So say something! You can't think of anything. Check to see which of the girls has bigger breasts. Wonder which one is hotter. Figure that it's probably the one you won't get. Which one will you get? There's no question—you want the gorgeous one. She'd never be into you. Look at her. No way! Maybe she would be. Maybe she is. She looks at you. She is! She looks at your friend. She's talking to him. She's not into you. Asshole! You can't believe you thought she'd be into you. Face it—you'll end up with the other one, you always do. Maybe you should just go for the other one right off, since you'll end up with her anyway. Wonder if you were just born to lose.

How to Die of Embarrassment

ON A DATE

Pick up a slice of pizza and take a bite. Watch the mozzarella cheese stretch. Bite down harder. It is still stretching. Move slice farther away from mouth. The strands are growing thinner and longer. You can see three spaghetti-like strands of mozzarella cheese extending out of your mouth. They are hanging between the slice and your mouth like jump ropes. You do not know what to do. With the hand that is not holding the pizza, grab cheese with fingers, break off, and stuff ends in mouth. Chew, swallow, do not look at date, and begin again.

IN THE YOUNG MEN'S DEPARTMENT

Your mother informs the salesman that you need a suit. It's for a very special occasion, next Saturday night, you have a date. "Mom, he doesn't care!" She keeps on talking. How many children does the salesman have? Isn't that funny, she has three, too—you are the oldest. You're very fussy when it comes to clothes. Is his son like that? "Mom, would you cut it out already!"

Veto several suits without giving a reason. Then find an acceptable jacket and try on the matching pants. Say that you don't like them, they itch. While your mother and the salesman comb the rack for another suit, notice two kids from your class in the next department. Your mother says, "Don't you know those boys?" Say, "No," and turn around so they can't see your face. Try on another suit and agree to buy it just to get out of the store. The fitter takes measurements. He marks the legs. Your mother advises him, "Don't make them too tight." People are looking. Now he's going to measure the inner seam from ankle to crotch. He's going to touch you. Are you going to get turned on? Everyone's looking. Worry.

BETWEEN CLASSES

On the way to your class on the third floor, detour down to the first floor to pass the room where he has his next class. Is he there? He is! Smile and say, "Hi." He says hi back. Ask if he did the English assignment. Ask if he's ready for the test. Say that you'll see him later. Smile and say, "Bye." He is so cute!

Continue down the hall, swinging your hips in a way that seems sexy. Then, as you start up the stairs to the second floor, start running. Just make it to class in time. Flop down in seat, drop books on floor, take mirror out of purse, and look at yourself. There's a piece of apple between your two front teeth.

AFTER PICKING UP A GIRL

Offer her a cigarette. She says no. Take one yourself, saying, "I really should quit." Tap cigarette on table to condense tobacco. Put cigarette in mouth, ignite lighter, and continue to talk for a moment with cigarette dangling from mouth and lighter lit. Pause, light

cigarette, inhale, and—what's the matter? Remove cigarette from mouth and examine it. You lit the filter end.

IN A FANCY RESTAURANT

Order steak tartare medium rare.

AT YOUR BOYFRIEND'S HOUSE FOR DINNER

Salad: With fork, pick up a piece of lettuce and look at it. Will it fit in your mouth? Put it back on the plate. Attempt to cut with fork. Wonder if it's okay to use a knife on salad. Look around the table to see if anyone else is using his knife. No one is. Pick up the lettuce again. Put it down. Pick it up. Put it down. Pick it up, open mouth, close eyes, and cram it in. Open eyes and realize that your boyfriend's mother is looking at you strangely. You are eating her salad.

Roll: Remembering what your mother told you about the correct way to eat rolls, break off a small piece, scattering crumbs on the table. Butter, place in mouth. While chewing, answer a question, spraying a shower of crumbs across the table.

(Alternative: Mistake roll for baked potato—cut slit in top and stuff butter in.)

AT THE BEACH

Drop purse on sand. Remove sandals and take off jeans. Pull T-shirt over head—you are in your bikini. Smile at him. Unfold the blanket, taking two corners and giving him two. Lower blanket onto sand. Flop down on your stomach and rest weight on elbows. Look down to check cleavage—the Kleenexes are showing.

AT HER FRONT DOOR

Should you ask her or just do it? Should you ask her or just do it? Should you ask her? Just do it. Move forward to kiss her and step on her foot.

ON THE TELEPHONE

"Doyouwanttogoonadate?"
"What?"
"Doyouwanttogoonadate?"
"What?"
"Doyouwanttogoona—who is this? Oh, I have the wrong number."

IN THE LINGERIE DEPARTMENT

Take bras into dressing room and close the curtain, trying to make sure that the curtain is pulled all the way across the top and that the sides of the curtain meet the sides of the door opening. The curtain gapes. Try to fix it, pulling it again at the top and sides. You can't fix it. Worry that someone can see in. Worry that the saleslady will come into the dressing room.

Work quickly, listening for voices. In the middle of fastening the first bra, look up. Someone has mistaken your dressing room for hers—oh, excuse me. Start to sweat. Try to fix the curtain again so it doesn't gape. You can't fix it. Slip on the next bra. "What?" The saleslady is peeking in. She wants to know how you're doing. You need help? You need anything else? Are you sure? She leaves. Try to fix the curtain. Worry that someone can see in. Worry that the saleslady will return. Work quickly.

IN A DRUGSTORE

After choosing a drugstore where nobody knows you . . .
After telling yourself that it's no big deal . . .
After telling yourself that you have a perfect right to buy them . . .
After standing at the magazine rack until all the other customers have left the store . . .
After looking at magazines until the woman is no longer behind the cash register—the man is . . .
After saying to yourself, "Okay, now!" . . .
After saying, "Okay, now!" three more times . . .
Leave.

IN THE BOYS' LOCKER ROOM

Is his bigger than yours? Look at it! It's huge! Gigantic! What about him? No, you don't think so, about the same, yeah, the same. What about him? Hmmmmmm. And him? No, yes, can't tell but with your luck, probably. Him, no; him, no; him, yes, definitely, absolutely, for sure. And him? And him? And him? And him?

IN THE HALLS

As agreed, meet your best friend for lunch at her locker. She says, "Don't look now but you've got your period."

How to Go on a Date

INSTRUCTIONS FOR GIRL

Look at the clock. In half an hour he'll be here. Ask your mother if your hair's okay. Ask her if your colors go together. Is she sure? Is she positive? Look in the mirror. Think that you look great. Think that you look terrible. What about your belt—should you wear it fastened in the center or slightly off to the side? Demonstrate the belt fastened both ways. Your mother says she doesn't see any difference—both ways look nice. "Mom, are you crazy, they don't!" Tell her she always says that. Tell her she never gives you any help. Tell her she's hopeless. Look in the mirror and experiment with the belt. It looks terrible! You look terrible!

Your mother says, "Relax—you look lovely." Inform her that you do not look lovely. How would she know, she can't even tell which way a belt looks best. Check the clock. In twenty more minutes he'll be here.

Consider the problem: Where should you be when he arrives? Should you answer the door? If you do, will he think you've been hanging around waiting for him? Maybe you should be on the telephone. That's good—then it would look like you're in the process of doing something and not totally focused on him. But suppose he thinks you're too busy? You know—you'll be in your room and have your mother answer the door. You can make an entrance. But if you make an entrance, that would be like it's really a date, and it's sort of a date but not really. Or is it? You can't decide. Anyway, it doesn't matter because if you make an entrance, he'll have to be alone with your parents, and you wouldn't wish that on your worst enemy. Then remember to stay away from windows so he can't see you when he walks up to the front door. Look at the clock.

Sit down on the living room couch, stretching body out almost horizontally in an attempt to keep your pants smooth and unwrinkled. What time is it? Oh God, it's almost time. Evaluate the living room furniture. Wish that it wasn't so nice; wish that it was nicer. Evaluate your mother. Why does she wear her hair that weird way? Look at her shoes—look at that, she's wearing slippers! When she gets up to walk across the room, say, "Mom, you have the biggest butt."

The doorbell!!!!!!!!!!!!!!!!!!!

On your way to answer it, pass your father in the hall. He's coming into the living room, and he is wearing his pajamas and robe. Oh no!

INSTRUCTIONS FOR BOY

Shake hands with her mother and father. Say hello to her sister. You do not know whether to sit or to remain standing.

While listening to your mother inquire what it's like out tonight, where your date lives, and what movie you're going to, think, Please God, let me get him out of here fast. Say that you'd better get going. Say that you'll be late. Hope that you can leave before your dad cracks one of his jokes. Inform your mother, in answer to her question, that you said you'll be home by twelve-thirty, you'll be home, and wonder why she had to bring it up again. Now she is suggesting that you wear a sweater. "Mom, I already told you, I don't need one."

The telephone is ringing. Your dad says it's probably for you, he's going to have to take a part-time job to pay your telephone bill. Very funny. On your way out the door, hear your dad call out, "Drive carefully." Why does he always say that! As soon as you are outside, tell date, "I don't know what's the matter with my parents, they're driving me crazy."

Tell her that her parents don't seem so bad, she should meet yours. Then wonder whether she expects you to open the car door for her. Open it; but feel ridiculous ending a sentence in the middle when you close the door and finishing it, as though there had been no break in conversation, after you walk around to your side and get in.

On the way to the movie, discuss the class you have together, referring to the teacher either by first name or nickname. For instance, if his name is Mr. Chester, call him Chester the Molester. Remember to slouch slightly lopsided in the car seat, recalling a movie in which the hero always had one shoulder higher than the other.

After speculating on the sex life of the French teacher, announce that you once counted all the *um*'s she said in one period and it came to one hundred thirty-six. Then add that you have this other teacher for geometry who writes everything he says on the blackboard. Like if he says, "There's a test tomorrow," he turns and writes "tomorrow" on the blackboard. Really. Say, "Oh, don't you hate it when someone scratches the blackboard with their fingers."

"You hate this?"—run fingernails across dashboard.

Shriek.

Crack up.

Beg him to stop, you absolutely can't bear it, don't do it again, please. Anyway these kids you know called up the geometry teacher at four in the morning and his wife answered.

Speculate on who would marry him, mentioning various animals, while you think, Thank goodness she talks a lot. Hope that she talks all night so you don't have to. Then remind yourself to look cool while you drive. Have one hand on the wheel and the other resting on the window ledge. When turning corners, use only one hand to turn steering wheel, letting wheel slide through fingers back into straight line once corner is turned. Hope that your date admires this technique. Then wonder what you could do to make her really like you, and decide to roll up your sleeves while you drive.

Oh God, that geometry teacher is so disgusting. You hear he dyes his hair because this other friend of yours saw him on a rainy day. His hair was gray in back and all this black stuff was on his shoulders. Immediately wish you hadn't said that—it sounded so dumb. God, was that dumb! Why did you say that? Why did you say that!

"He probably combs his hair with shoe polish."

"What?" You weren't listening. You were thinking how dumb you are. Lame. A jerk. You can never keep your trap shut. Your date hates you—you know it.

"I said he probably combs his hair with shoe polish."

Smile at his joke while you think he hates you for sure. You blew it, you know it, you blew it.

Do an imitation of the geometry teacher in a lavatory asking if he can borrow someone's shoe polish—he forgot his and he needs to comb his hair.

Start laughing.

Pretend to comb hair with shoe-polish applicator.

"Oh God, please stop, please, oh please, please, I can't stop, oh my stomach, my stomach, my stomach! Oh please!" Clutch stomach and be unable to stop laughing. Gasp that you heard about someone who laughed so hard while he was eating that a French fry came out of his nose.

Pretend to blow nose, say, "Want a fry?" and offer date the contents of your hand.

Say, "Oh no!" "Please stop!" and "Oh my stomach," and start
laughing all over again. Then wonder if your eyeliner is running and
stop laughing. Sit up straight, touch finger gingerly to edges of eyes to
pick up any excess liner.

> *She thinks you're funny. She thinks you are really funny! Great.*
> *Signal, pull into theater parking lot, and wonder if tonight you'll get it.*

II

> *You bet you do, you know it, you're going to get it. Hey, hey, hey,*
> *tonight's the night, you feel it in your bones. Bones? Not bad! That's*
> *where you feel it all right. Or, you should say, bone! Check out your*
> *reflection in the glass of the ticket booth. Then, on the way to join date*
> *at the end of the ticket holders' line, see if you know anyone the two of*
> *you could butt in front of, and call yourself an asshole—if you don't*
> *stop thinking about getting it, you'll jinx it. Stop thinking, I know it,*
> *I'm going to get it, and consider instead what you could say to your*
> *date that would really help you get it for sure, like a compliment. As*
> *soon as you see her, ask if she did something to her hair—it looks*
> *different.*
>
> *That wasn't good enough. Add that her sweater looks really good*
> *and wish that you were the type of guy who could lay it on thick.*

He gave you a compliment. He likes you! He's attracted to you! Do
not say thank you. Respond, "Yeah, a turtleneck for a turtle," and

immediately wish you could take it back. You did it again! Why did you say that? Why did you say that!!!!!!!!

You and your big mouth—why can't you act normal? You wish you knew. What's the matter with you, anyway? Now he absolutely knows you're a complete creep. Think to yourself, Now I blew it for sure, while you say out loud that you hope there are coming attractions, you just love coming attractions.

"What? What did you say?" You didn't hear because it just occurred to you that while waiting in the ticket holders' line, you might get an erection.

"I said I hope there are coming attractions."

"Oh yeah, me too." Tell yourself to stop thinking about it—if you think about an erection, you are certain to get one. Continue to think about it as the line files into the theater, and take advantage of this opportunity to touch your date for the first time: Put your hand on her shoulder to guide her in. You are relieved that, as soon as you sit down, the theater lights go down.

Do not put on your glasses. Consider it for a moment but decide that you would rather not see the movie than have him see you in glasses. Squint. As the theater gets dark and the main attraction starts, say, "Oh great, coming attractions!" and realize that you made a mistake. Hope that your date didn't hear you.

"What?" You are still thinking about an erection.　　73

"Nothing."

What to do with your hands while watching the movie: Cross arms in front of chest and tuck hands under.

Uncross arms—your date won't be able to hold your hand if he can't find it.

Clasp hands together in lap.

This doesn't feel right either. It feels so prissy. Unclasp hands.

Now your hands are lying in your lap, ready, available. Who sits with their hands like this? How embarrassing. This is ridiculous. You know he knows you're leaving your hands out in the open in case he wants one. Suppose he doesn't want one?

Shift in your chair as if to get more comfortable and take her hand at the same time, as if the entire movement were one. This action should be accomplished with eyes glued to screen, giving the impression that the head does not know and is not aware of what the body is doing.

Pay equal attention to watching the movie and stroking her hand. After a while, switch from just clasping her hand to intertwining your fingers with hers. Hmmmmmm, that was easy. Continue to stroke her hand, moving your thumb back and forth across hers. Things are going great—you're better at this than you thought! Switch her hand to your other hand, and put now-free arm around her: Begin by laying it down on the back of her chair and slowly easing it onto her shoulders. While stroking her arm and shoulder with one hand and her hand with the other, imagine seeing your friend tomorrow and saying, "She went down like a sub." Imagine saying that she couldn't get enough. Imagine not saying anything to your friend, just winking at him. Gloat

at the idea; then realize that your hand, the one that is holding hers, is sweating. It's practically dripping. It's disgusting!

Change from intertwining your fingers with hers to clasping her hand again. This doesn't help—your hand is getting wetter. You are dying to wipe it off. Should you? If you do, will you be able to get her hand back? Suppose she won't give it to you? Worry about this as hand continues to sweat.

Change from intertwining your fingers with his to clasping his hand again. Your hand is dripping wet. You are dying to wipe it off. Should you? If you do, will he take your hand again? While worrying about this, realize that the armrest is jabbing into your side. You are leaning into it so you can be close to your date while his arm is around you. Move slightly in seat to get more comfortable. You hear a squeaky sound. What was that? Oh, the leather seat made a noise when you moved. Suppose your date thinks that noise was you farting. Move slightly again so he realizes it was not a fart but the seat. Do it again. There. Your hand is still sweating. Your side is killing you. You do not know what to do.

Working quickly—release her hand, rub sweaty hand dry on pants leg while pretending to pull up sock, grasp her hand again.

Working quickly—when he releases your hand, wedge purse against armrest for a cushion, wiping hand off on purse in the process; grasp his hand again.

Now repeat, following all instructions beginning on page 74 with "Pay equal attention to watching the movie and stroking her hand," and ending with "grasp her hand again."

III

"What do you want to eat?"

"I don't know, what do you want to eat?" Study the menu while twirling a piece of your hair around and around with your index finger. Pull the strand away from your head and try to see it out of the corner of your eye. Then move strand over in front of face and place end in mouth. Notice what you are doing—you are chewing your hair. Stop immediately and brush hair back with hand. Study the menu. You don't know what to have. What do you think he's going to order? Try to figure it out so you can order the same thing. "What are you having?"

"I don't know, what are you having?"

"I don't know."
When the waitress comes for your order, tell him to go first, you can't decide, and then order the same thing. The waitress wants to know how you'd both like it.

"Medium rare."

"Medium rare."
That's amazing—you both like your cheeseburgers the same way. You bet it's a sign. Now she wants to know what you'll have on it.

"Everything."

"Everything."

That really is eerie—the two of you have exactly the same taste in cheeseburgers! You know it's a sign—it has to be. You are soulmates! Smile at him.

Wish that you hadn't ordered "everything" because of the onion and look around for the waitress—should you change your order? Forget it, you can't, your date will know why. Look at your date. She is smiling at you. Is she laughing at you? Perhaps there's a booger hanging out of your nose.

You know, you two really are a lot alike. It's amazing, it really is. Do you think he really likes you? Suppose he does. Think, Please God, make him like me, make him like me really a lot. I really want him to. What if he said he loved you? Imagine it—he falls in love with you. Then imagine telling your best friend all about the date tomorrow. Oh God, tomorrow! You don't want it to come. You don't want the date to end. Oh, please don't end; don't end, ever.

You are absolutely certain there is a booger hanging out of your nose. Casually put finger lengthwise under nose and flick it back and forth for a second as though you have an itch, but actually to ascertain if something weird is hanging there.

Notice his hands as he rubs his nose. He has beautiful hands. A guy's hands are really important. Next to eyes, you like hands the most. If there's one thing you hate, it's guys with fat, stubby fingers.

Look around the restaurant at the other couples. Wonder if people
are looking at the two of you as a couple. Hope that they are.

*Out of sight, under the table, wipe finger on pants. Did anything
come off? Look down, then look up quickly to see if your date had any
idea what you were doing. Smile at her.*

Smile at him. He is soooooo cute!

Smile back, flipping your fork up and down.

Stop meeting his eye: Look down at your paper placemat and fold
the edge of it over and over.

*Bang the bowl of a spoon with your fork to try to flip it into the air.
Notice what you are doing and stop. Put down fork and try desperately
to think of something to say.*

Run your finger along the edge of the placemat, tracing its rim.
Appear to be fascinated by the rim. Appear to study its every curve
and turn while you worry—I can't think of anything to say. I knew
this would happen. I knew it, I knew it, I knew it!

*You know you heard a joke last week in school—now what was it?
Who told it to you? Oh yeah, him. What was it? Pick up fork and flap
it up and down in your hand. What was it? Put fork down. Try to
remember. Pick it up, you can't remember, put it down, put hands in
lap, put hands back on table, pick up knife and twirl it. What was it?*

Shit, you can't remember! Stop twirling knife—you just realized that you can see your reflection in the knife blade. Sort of. Check it out. Try to see yourself, moving your face a bit to get the complete picture in pieces. Then continue twirling. What was that joke? What was that joke? You know it—you're going to blow it. If you don't think of something to say soon, she'll never do it.

Stop studying the placemat and instead look curiously and intently around the restaurant. Scrutinize the people at the next table. Scrutinize the pictures on the walls. Pray: Please God, please let me think of something to say. Please, I'll do anything, just let me think of something. Oh, this is unreal! I knew this would happen. I knew it and I was right! Oh God, please!!! I'll never ask for anything else, just let me have this, please. This is awful. This is the worst! Suppose the entire rest of the date goes by and I can't think of anything. Suppose I have to sit here in silence. I'll die, I'll absolutely die. Oh God, please!!!!!!

> *Without advance warning, commence impersonation of Steve Martin.*

You do not have any idea what your date is doing. Smile as if you know. What is he talking about? Oh, it's a routine. When he's done, tell him that was great. Ask who it was.

> *Immediately upon ending impersonation of Martin, commence a Richard Pryor routine. Perform without looking date in eye. Finish, lift Coca-Cola glass, and say, "Here's looking at you, kid."*

Smile and laugh even though he's mumbling and you can't hear very well. You do not know exactly how to react. When he says, "Here's looking at you, kid," hope that the couple at the next table are not watching.

Do not finish your cheeseburger even if you want to.

Do not go to the bathroom even if you have to.

IV

Open and close the front door very gently. Listen. Are your parents up? No sound. Their light is out. Remove shoes and tiptoe past their room. You made it. "Is that you?" Shit, they're up. "Yeah, it's me, Mom, I'm home." Quickly go to your bedroom and close the door.

Drop shoes on floor, flop onto your back on the bed, and stare at the ceiling. Close your eyes. Take a deep breath, in-out, very slowly. You're in love. You are. You are absolutely madly, passionately in love. Think about the scene in the car. Heavy. Oh God, you are so turned on! "What????????" Sit up. Your father has just opened the door. While he yells, "Do you know what time it is, young lady?" "It's two o'clock—where the hell were you?" "What the hell's going on?" and "Who do you think you are?" as well as "I was worried sick and so was your mother," shout back at him, "Take it easy," "Jeez, God," "I wasn't doing anything," "I wasn't anywhere," and "If you'd just looked outside and down the block, you would have seen me. I was just sitting in his car—*talking!*" Then think that it's your dad's fault that you're lying, not yours. Also scream that he acts like you're a criminal or something.

Your mother has just appeared. She is telling your father to calm down, you'll discuss it in the morning. They leave.

Thank God! Walk over to the mirror and look at your face. It's flushed. Oh God, it was so incredible! Sit down on the bed. With your finger, trace your date's initials on the bedspread. Smile and gaze at

82

the place on the bedspread where the initials would be if you could
see them. Close your eyes—you are back in the car. Open them. You
are in your room. Think about your parents. They're driving you
crazy.

When she closes her front door, turn and walk back to the car. Shit!
You didn't get it.
You knew you wouldn't, you never get it. Everyone always gets it but

*you. Get into the car and slam the door. Start it while complaining to
yourself:*

*If she doesn't put out, then why did that other guy say . . . Do you
think she was telling the truth? Oh, who knows? "I can't handle
it"—that's what she said. "I really want it to be right the first time."
Shit. Shit, shit, shit. Add up how much money you spent. Movie,
cheeseburger, parking. A fortune and you didn't get it. Sucker. Do
you think she'll do it next week? Pray—"Oh God, I'll do anything, just
make her do it." Suppose she won't even go out with you again.*

Suppose she doesn't like you. That's why she didn't do it, she doesn't like you. She thinks you're boring, ugly, a creep. She's right, you are a creep. You blew it, you know it. Think, Oh God, she's got to like me. She's got to! You'd better say you love her. Next week, you'd better say more of that stuff in general. Why didn't you? Jerk, that's all it would have taken, you know.

What's the matter with you anyway?

While driving, tilt the rearview mirror toward you to get a quick look at yourself. Make a face into the mirror, thinking, Jerkhead, you didn't get it; then inadvertently start grinning, thinking, Yeah, you didn't get it but you almost got it. Pretty close. You were fuckin' freakin' out there for a while—you couldn't believe it. You almost had her convinced. Not bad. You are not bad at all. Next week you'll get it. For sure.

Imagine seeing your friend tomorrow and saying, "She went down like a sub." Imagine not saying anything, just winking. Think, Yeah, that's what I'll do. Well, why not?—I almost got it.

Drive home.

Masturbate.

How to Worry

Worry that if you neck too much, you'll get mononucleosis.
Worry that if you masturbate, you'll get pimples.
Worry that if you masturbate, you'll get brain damage.
Worry that if you masturbate, you'll go blind.
Worry that, while making out, you ought to be talking too, saying encouraging things like "Oh baby!"
Worry that in a long kiss, you'll have to breathe through your nose and your nose will be stopped up.
Worry that your breath smells.
Worry that you have B.O.
Worry that everyone is in on the joke but you.
Worry that there's a right way to dress and you don't know it.
Worry that there's a right way to neck and you don't know it.
Worry that there's a right way to fuck and you don't know it.
Worry that your date will be able to tell that you don't know.
If you are a girl, worry that your breasts are too round. Worry that your breasts are too pointed. Worry that your nipples are the wrong color. Worry that your breasts point in different directions.
If you are a boy, worry that you will get breasts.
Worry that your nose is too fat. Worry that your nose is too long. Worry that your neck is too fat. Worry that your lips are too fat.

Worry that your ass is too fat. Worry that your ears stick out. Worry that your eyebrows are too close together.

If you are a boy, worry that you'll never be able to grow a mustache.

If you are a girl, worry that you have a mustache.

Worry that you won't like the food at other people's houses.

Worry that you will eat too much food at other people's houses.

Worry that when you go to the bathroom, people will hear. Worry that the lock on the door doesn't work. Worry that someone will walk in.

Worry that everyone hates you.

Worry that everyone thinks you're stupid.

Worry that you have ugly toes.

How to Be an Older Brother

You and your sister are in a restaurant. The waiter has not come to your table yet. He's taking orders at the table next to yours. Whisper:

"Hey, that waiter's pretty cute, don't you think? Not bad, not bad at all. Look at that bod." Raise your voice. "Want to meet him? You sure? Look, I'll be happy to introduce you. Really, it's no trouble. Hey waiter, waiter, my sister wants to meet you. Take it easy, it's okay, the waiter doesn't mind. He thinks you're cute, too. Don't you?"

You are in the living room. Your sister's date has just arrived. Introduce yourself and invite him to have a seat:

"My sister tells me you're a junior. Don't you think she's a little young for you? Never mind, just kidding. What does your father do? What do you plan to be when you grow up? Is college contemplated? What are you going to major in? Are you two doing it?—just kidding."

When your sister walks in, tell her you were having a little talk with her, ah, friend. Tell the guy, "Take good care of her." Say to them both, "Have fun, kids." Tell him to get her home early, you don't like her gallivanting around 'til all hours. Wink at him.

It's late at night. You have just arrived home from a date. Your sister returned from hers already. Knock on her bedroom door:

"Hi. Have fun?" Sit down in a chair, put legs up on desk. Stretch. "Tell you what—I'll tell you everything that happened on my date if you tell me everything that happened on yours. All the juicy details, okay? Great—you go first."

When she's finished and it's your turn, say, "Sucker."

You are sitting at the dinner table with your mom, your dad, and your sister:

"My little sister had quite a time last night." Poke her. "Didn't you? She told me all about it. Didn't you? Yesirree, quite a time. What?—don't kick me under the table. I told you I wouldn't tell. You can trust me. I mean, jeez, do you think I'd tell what you and that guy—well, I wouldn't, I just wouldn't. You can trust me—I'm your older brother, aren't I? Would I tell? Besides, do you think I'd want Mom and Dad to freak?"

Your sister had a date last night:

Wink at her. "Wearing a turtleneck, I see. Mom, have you ever noticed that every time she goes out with that guy, she wears a turtleneck the next day?"

Your sister is in the living room, talking to a boy. She introduces you:

"Mark? This is Mark! Well, well, well. Excuse me, Mark, is that a pimple or did you cut yourself shaving?"

The telephone rings:

"Hello. You want to speak to my sister?" Hold the receiver up high so she can't grab it. "Are you sure you want to speak to her? Okay, if you're sure. Who's calling?—no wait, let me guess. Richard? Not Richard! Jeff? Steve? Then who is it? David! Well, what do you know! My sister told me all about you. We were so worried you wouldn't call. What a relief, you finally called her. What took you so long?

The telephone rings:

"Hello. You want to speak to my sister? Who's calling? David. Again! Well, David, I'm sorry to be the one to break the news but she was just run over by a garbage truck."

The telephone rings:

"Who calling? Rick. Gee, Rick, you'll have to wait a minute. She's going to the bathroom right now."

How to Go Steady

Dear Diary,

Good news! Judi found out! She asked Wendy to ask Michelle to ask Jennifer to ask Doug if he was interested in me. If he thought I was cute, etc., etc., etc., and he said—are you ready, diary?—"Yes!" Naturally Jennifer told him I was interested back. Anyway, I am going to see him this weekend at the party. Seth's parents are going away so we are all going over there.

DD,

I can't believe it—Denise wasn't invited to Seth's and I was. If she knew, would she be upset! I'd never tell, that's for sure. All week I was so worried that Denise would ask what I was doing Saturday but it's already Friday and so far so good. I feel so bad for her. Judi and I discussed whether we should ask Seth to ask Denise to the party. We talked to Michelle about it. Michelle says that guys just don't like Denise, and if she did go she probably wouldn't have a good time, so it would be better not to. I guess there's nothing I can do.

Oh Doug, I hope you like me. I can't wait to see you. Time, please go fast.

DD,

It's very late—2:30 a.m.!!—but I can't sleep. I had to write. It was incredible. We talked all night. Doug's really interesting. He plays the guitar. He's really into it. He especially likes the Grateful Dead because he says they stand for something. He really respects them. He says they're not just in it for the money. I felt like we really communicated.

I hope he didn't think I was a jerk, or real boring, or anything. Oh diary, I think something is happening. At last! I thought my whole life I'd just be guys' friends—always a friend, never a girlfriend. Do you think Doug could, does he really . . . ? I hope so. Doug said he'd call this week and maybe we'd go to a concert. He kissed me— actually we kissed quite a lot. Do you know what he said after he kissed me the first time? He said, in this really pleased voice, "Allllllllllll right!" We frenched—his tongue is smooth and doesn't have any little bumps or anything. Also he did this weird thing where he ran his tongue across my gums—sounds disgusting? Diary, you are a real prude. I think Doug kisses like a thirty-year-old.

Tonight I shall hug my pillow and pretend that it is Doug and we are locked in a permanent embrace—'til death do us part. Goodnight, dear diary, dearest diary, sweet dreams.

DD,

This is what I did today—lay on the bed and stared. I'm in a trance. All I can think about is Douglas. I close my eyes and we're kissing again. It feels like we really are, especially in my stomach, isn't that strange? There's this funny feeling like jumps—well, I can't describe it, diary, but you'd know it if you had it. Anyway, I keep imagining

that Doug and I are sitting on the bed together, locked in passion, kissing, kissing, kissing, and then we start to fall over, and that's the end of my fantasy, ha ha. I wonder what happens next!!!!!!!!!

Judi says she's positive Doug really likes me. Seth told her that Doug told him after the party that he thought he was going to go with me next. Lucky me! It's going to happen, diary, I am going to have a boyfriend.

I think Judi's going to be going with Seth soon 'cause at the party they made out all over the place.

DD,

Oh boy, was I nervous because it had been three days since the party and no call from Doug. I was worried that he lost the phone number but he couldn't have lost it because he wrote it on his jeans. I thought maybe his mom put them in the washing machine and the ink came off. Anyway, today Doug stopped by after school, and now the person who is writing to you has a boyfriend. Can you tell from my penmanship?

It was really scary 'cause at the last minute I thought maybe it wouldn't happen. We were in the living room, he kissed me, and I almost died—there was a hair in my mouth. I didn't know what to do. I sort of casually brushed my hair back from my face but it was still there!!!!!!!! I froze. I was thinking, it's over for sure. He's going to leave. He's going to think he made a giant mistake in liking me and he'll leave. But he didn't. Then I brushed my hair back again and the hair came out. Doug told me that before Seth's party he thought he didn't want another girlfriend but now maybe he did after all. I was so happy. I told him I really like him but I didn't want to be hurt. (I almost said the way I was with Jeffrey, but he didn't know about Jeffrey, and I'd die if he did.)

Doug only smokes Marlboro. He says they have the best taste. We talked about Kenny, who is sort of his friend but not really. Kenny is always trying to be cool so he buys Marlboro but he doesn't even buy them in the hard pack, and then he goes around thinking, I'm so cool, I smoke Marlboro, when he's really not 'cause he doesn't even know how to buy them.

After Doug left, I saved the butts from the ashtray. I shall never throw them away.

DD,

We thought she didn't but she did. Denise called Judi's Saturday night and her mom said she was out. We didn't know because Judi's mom forgot to tell her, so today Denise asked Judi where she was and Judi wasn't going to tell her but she did. Then Denise called me and said she didn't care anyway, she didn't want to go, that those kids were morons, and that I'd really changed 'cause I was getting like them. If that's the way she feels, I'm not speaking to her. I talked to Judi about it, and she says that she's not speaking to Denise either. It's Denise's own fault—she has too many zits and if she'd just use Clearasil, she'd look a lot better, but she won't.

DD,

Mom's furious. I put my retainer in my lunch bag and threw it away by mistake.

DD,

It's so funny. I thought when school started, I'd puke if I had to go. I was so totally depressed at the thought. But diary, it's different now. Judi is still my first best friend, but I'm also friends with Wendy, Jennifer (who I never thought would speak to me), Michelle, and even Sheila a little. I have to admit it, diary, I've changed. Today Judi and Wendy were talking to Seth and Russell, and I came up behind Russell and put my hands over his eyes. "Guess who?" I said. I am definitely learning how to flirt and I guess it shows.

Oops, there's Doug on the t-phone or the tee-hee phone as Judi calls it. Talk to you later.

DD,

I never thought it could be like this. Doug and I are totally in sync. We both like jamoca almond fudge ice cream and pizza plain, just with extra cheese. Saturday, when we were getting pizza after an entire afternoon spent in the car (where else!), Doug said, "What's your favorite kind?" I was sort of embarrassed because I just like it plain with extra cheese, but he said, "I don't believe it!" Also Doug is totally into unicorns, which I am too. He knows exactly what I mean when I say, "There's only one unicorn!"

By the way, Judi read this book that says if a guy's fingers and toes are long that means his you-know-what is, too. Don't be shocked, DD, these are simply the facts of life though I have yet to verify them from personal experience. Oh well, I'm still young. Gotta go. Haven't finished my English assignment in *Tale of Two Cities*. Judi calls it "Sale of Two Titties"!!?!

DD,

Debra makes me sick. She's such a phony. I've really never met anyone so conceited. I don't know why guys don't see through her.

DD,

I've just hung up from talking to Douglas (I think I like the name Douglas better than Doug). He played the guitar to me over the phone. It was so beautiful. Doug and Tom are thinking of forming a band. They both play guitar and Doug says that all they need is a bass and drums. I said I'd play the cymbals, ha ha. They are going to meet at Tom's tomorrow to discuss it.

Doug thinks that even though Seth likes Judi, he also likes Wendy, and that Judi's chasing him, and he's fed up, and she'd better watch out. I don't know if I should tell Judi. Maybe not. Doug thinks Debra is a phony too. He says she just gets guys to go with her and then she drops them on their heads.

Tonight Douglas and I had a record phone call—four hours. Tomorrow we are going to stay on the phone all night. I'll get in bed and put the receiver under my ear against the pillow and so will Doug. Then we can sleep together. Sexy, huh? I hope he doesn't snore!

DD,

Russell is having a party after all. He wasn't going to but then he changed his mind. Seth is taking Judi but she may not go. She's really upset. She has a giant zit between her eyebrows. Russell says that

99

since Doug is his best friend, Doug and I get one bedroom (ooo la la!). Russell and Debra get the other. Doug's going to bring his guitar. He has a book, *The Prophet,* by an ancient philosopher. He says it's full of really great stuff and he and Tom are going to set some of it to music. They are thinking of going professional after high school.

DD,

Today I am very depressed. I just feel sad. From the moment I woke up, I wanted to cry. Why? I don't understand. I have a boyfriend. Most kids think I'm cute. I'm pretty popular—not as popular as Jennifer or Sheila but they're probably the most. I'll never be popular like them in a million years. I do okay in school. So why am I so unhappy? Why do I feel like crying? Oh diary, I wish I knew.

DD,

Listen to this—Russell's party was a mess. Seth took Judi but then he went outside and necked with Wendy. I didn't even know about it because Doug and I were you-know-where. But then Russell's parents came home and we had to tear out of the bedroom really fast. Doug left his guitar on the bed so we thought they'd know for sure. Oh diary, I'm going so fast because you won't believe what happened. As soon as I got home I called Judi. She was crying. She said she hated Seth and if he died, she wouldn't care. I said I thought Seth was really terrible and I was going to call Doug and tell him so he would tell Seth. I told her what Doug said about Seth's thinking that she was chasing him. I was just trying to help and you know what she said?—ever since I was going with Douglas, all I ever said was what Doug said, and that Doug was as much of a jerk as Seth. She said I thought I was so great because I was going with Doug. I said I didn't think I was so great. I don't, diary. I don't think I act so great or anything. Anyway I know I'm right because I asked Jennifer and she said that Judi has an inferiority complex—that's why she chases guys.

I'm never speaking to Judi again. She can find another best friend for all I care. She thinks she knows everything. She's really just a fake stuck-up. It's not my fault that I have a boyfriend and she doesn't.

Today Wendy called. She said that she really likes Seth and that she and Seth and Doug and I should double next week.

DD,

A very important issue is weighing on my mind. Can a person get pregnant without doing it? Specifically, can sperms travel through underpants. If you get them on your hand and touch yourself, can they swim up you? When two people lie close together, can they seep through from one to the other? What about if you swallow them? I suppose, diary, you realize that these are not hypothetical questions (except the last).

Once I heard that one in 200 could get pregnant without doing it. If this is true, I may be a dead duck. Just my luck to be pregnant and still a virgin. No one, but no one, would believe me!!!!!!!!!!!!!!

101

DD,

Today Judi and Jennifer were over and Doug and Tom stopped by on their way to practice. I think Tom likes Judi and definitely vice-versa. Jennifer says the reason Debra is so revolting is that she's spoiled rotten. No matter what she wants, her parents buy it for her. Her clothes cost a fortune. Debra always says things like "Oh really," only she says it in this la-de-da voice. Then she looks up at guys with these moony eyes. I think she looks like a cow but guys eat it up sideways. I don't get it. If I acted like that around guys, I would feel like a total jerk.

Jennifer's thinking of having a big party at the beach this summer. I said I thought it was a great idea but, diary, I don't know if I would go 'cause of how my legs look in a bathing suit.

DD,

Our two-month anniversary. Can it have really been this long? It feels like forever. Doug came over and brought me a rose.

DD,

Doug thinks we should do it. He's already done it. I don't know—I can't make up my mind. We've done everything but. Doug says it's one of life's greatest experiences.

To be or not to be, that is the question (hee hee hee). Oh God, tell me what to do. If I am going to lose my virginity, I guess I might as well lose it with Douglas. First of all, I love him. Second of all, he's already done it. Imagine what it would be like if we were both virgins! Judi knows about this couple that were both virgins and when they did it, he went in the wrong hole and got stuck! Anyway, I'm probably not a virgin technically. A person can lose her virginity from bicycle-riding, horseback-riding, or volleyball. Besides, does it really matter whether I'm a virgin (well, except maybe to Mom and Dad). Who can tell? Russell says he can spot a virgin a mile away. He says virgins walk differently from non-virgins.

I just can't decide. On the one hand, what am I waiting for? On the other hand, it's sort of like piercing your ears. Once you do it, you can't go back. Is the time right? Oh diary, I wish you could tell me what to do.

DD,

Mom read you!!!!!!!!! I don't believe it. I can't stand it. How could she do this to me! More later. Gotta go.

DD,

I can't believe it—my own personal private thoughts VIOLATED. I've never been so insulted in my life. Never! I won't trust her again, that's for sure. It was absolutely none of her business. None, none, none. What was she doing nosing around in my room? She said she wasn't nosing around, she was just putting some clean underwear in the drawer. Sure!!!!!!!!!! Fat chance! I wouldn't nose around in her room. She said if I didn't want her to read it, I wouldn't have left it where she could find it. I didn't! Honestly I can't stand it when she does something and then explains how it's really my fault. I'm never going to be such a hypocrite when I grow up.

Then she said she wanted to discuss it with me. Discuss "IT." Do I really think I'm old enough? After I do "IT," I might regret "IT" and then what? Good grief. All she ever thinks about is sex. She said she was at least relieved that I realize my parents care whether I'm a virgin. Then she asked if I wanted to see her gynecologist!!!!!!!!!!!!!!

Judi said it was the most disgusting thing she ever heard, and if I wanted to sleep at her house tonight, I could.

DD,

Sometimes I think Doug loves his guitar more than he loves me.

DD,

Today I was discussing my feelings about the guitar with Judi and she said that the guitar is a fallic (sp?) symbol. Judi says that lots of things are fallic symbols, not just flagpoles and guns. If this is true, it goes a long way to explaining why Doug takes his guitar everywhere —and I do mean everywhere.

DD,

I am so upset. Doug and I had a fight. It was awful. He was over, and he was just playing the guitar and not saying anything. Finally I asked him if something was wrong, and he said, "Can't a person just think once in a while!" He was really mad. Honestly, I was just asking. I said he was sorta moody. He was, diary, he was just staring into space. He said he wasn't moody, he was thinking about something. So then I said was he sure it wasn't me? He said to lay off. Then right afterward he left. He said he had to go somewhere and that it wasn't me—but suppose it was? Oh diary, what did I do? I thought everything was so great and now look what happens. Do you think it really wasn't me? Do you think everything's okay? Oh, please don't let it be me, please.

DD,

I'm scared to write this—if I do, will it come true? I think something is wrong between Doug and me. I'm not sure. Three nights ago he didn't call. The next day I waited at school for him in the usual place and he came by and said he'd call me later, he had to go practice with Tom. I thought he was kinda cold, but I kept telling myself it's probably my imagination. That was Friday. It's Sunday now and he still hasn't called. All weekend he didn't! Do you think he went out with someone else?

God, make him call. I want him to so much. Don't let it be over.

Maybe his grandmother died and that's why he didn't call. She's really old. Also she's a really bad driver and could have had an accident. Maybe, maybe, maybe.

DD,

Doug didn't call. I know it's over. I know it. Over. It can't be. It just can't be. Judi came over today and we talked.

105

DD,

I haven't written for a week. I just couldn't. I guess, dear diary, you'll understand when I tell you that Douglas and I broke up. Remember I told you he hadn't been calling. I wasn't sure if something was wrong. I mean it sort of seemed like it but I couldn't tell. Well, finally, I called him. I tried to be casual. I mean, if everything was okay between us, it would be perfectly natural for me to call him, wouldn't it? I just said, "Hi, what's happening?" He said, "Nothing." He was so cold I couldn't believe it. I said, "What have you been doing?" "Hanging around." "How's the band?" "Fine." I didn't know what to do, so please, diary, don't be mad at me, but I said, "I haven't seen you for ages." I guess it was a completely dumb thing to say. So then he said—oh diary, it makes me have tears in my eyes just to tell you. He said, "Look, I think we should just be friends."

I can't even express it, it hurts so much. I love him. I'll never love anyone else. Two whole months. Two beautiful, perfect months. Doug, why? Why don't you love me? I keep going over it. What happened? What did I do?

Do you think he loves someone else? Debra? Not Debra, please, anyone but Debra. I'll die if he loves her. I'm too scared to ask Judi.

I was thinking. Maybe I could stay in my room for the rest of the semester. Judi could bring me my homework and I could take absentee finals. I'll ask Mom. I don't think I can go to school anymore. This week was too terrible. I can't see him again. I just can't.

DD,

I saw Doug today. I went the long way to English so I would pass him going to social studies, and there he was. I thought my heart would stop. He said, "Hi." Do you think it meant something? All day I was wondering, what did it mean? Do you think he wants to go back?

DD,

I am sitting here looking at the telephone. I'm thinking of calling Doug. I almost did—I dialed but kept my finger right over the button on the phone and pressed it down the minute someone answered. I didn't even wait to see who it was. Oh diary, I wish he'd call me. I wish he'd say he made a mistake and he wanted to go back. Oh Doug, why? Why don't you love me? Is it because I'm a clod and always do dumb things. Like the time I was clicking my retainer, and he looked over, and it was half-way out of my mouth. Or in the restaurant when I put my retainer on the napkin. Everyone saw—it was so disgusting. Or the time the hair was in my mouth. I know that's why. I wish I knew how to do things right. Today I made a list of the questions I would ask Doug if I could talk to him. One, do you think I'm a jerk? Two, did you lie when you said you liked me? Three, why did you hurt me? This afternoon I imagined that when I came out of geometry, he'd be there. He'd look into my eyes. We'd be back together.

Oh Douglas, why???????????? I hate you. You and your dumb, stupid guitar. You and your group. I hope you get hit by a car. I hope you get electrocuted. I wouldn't care if you dropped dead. Boy, I sure am glad I didn't do it.

DD,

This is very important. I need you to tell me the honest-to-God truth. Do you think I should have done it? I should have, you're right. I should have done it and gotten it over with. Then at least I would have done it. But if I did it and he left me . . . I'm glad I didn't do it. I definitely shouldn't have. But maybe he wouldn't have left me . . . Oh that's dumb. But maybe he was right—I was a jerk not to do it. Suppose I never get another chance? I'll be the only person who wants to do it but no one wants to do it with her. I'll spend the rest of my life a virgin. It's my mom's fault. If she hadn't found you, diary, I would have done it for sure. She's always messing me up. I can't stand it—she's ruining my life!

DD,

I can't think about anyone but you-know-who. Why did he leave me? Why did he leave me! I can't bear it.

Do you think I will ever find anyone who loves me as much as I love him?

DD,

Don't faint. Doug is going with Jennifer!!!!!!!!! Judi told me. She said that she had to tell me 'cause she's my best friend and she didn't want me to hear it from someone else. I think I'm going to die.

DD,

Today Judi came over. She said that Michelle said that Wendy said that Johnny Buckley (as opposed to Johnny Gluck who is in my English class and a real creep) thinks I'm cute!!!!!!!!!